Write Your Story!

Includes Words of Encouragement

Studio Griffin
A Publishing Company
www.studiogriffin.net

For information, contact:
Studio Griffin
A Publishing Company
Garner, North Carolina
studiogriffin@outlook.com
www.studiogriffin.net

Cover Design by Ruth E. Griffin
Photo by © Adobe / Brian Jackson

First Edition

ISBN: 978-1-954818-37-8

1 2 3 4 5 6 7 8 9 10

One of the most frequently asked questions when it comes to the writing process is, "Where do I begin?" The best answer isn't as complicated as you might think:

Just start writing!

Remove the self-imposed roadblocks, get your favorite writing pen, and open up the 'Authors Up Journal' you've invested in. That's all you need to do to prepare yourself for what could be the most exhilarating journey of your life.

What you write IN can be just as important as the words you write down. The 'Authors Up Journal' gives you the space you need to tell your story, along with quotes to keep you motivated and encouraged.

You know you have it in you and there's no time like the present. So if you think you're ready, you just have one more thing to do:

Turn the page and write!

If you're waiting for the best time to write, that time is now!

RUTH E. GRIFFIN

Asking questions is not a sign of incompetence. It is a tool of the intelligent to discover the unknown.

ANDREA L. HINES

Cry, scream, and yell, but don't stop moving forward.

VICTORIA E. HENDERSON

The most influential conversation you will ever have is the one you have with yourself.

ANDREA L. HINES

You don't have to have everything figured out when you start—you just have to start. You will figure things out as you go.

RUTH E. GRIFFIN

I have to believe
that all is working
for my good. I
have to walk in
faith and not
doubt that He will
reward me as I
diligently seek Him.

VICTORIA E. HENDERSON

You can edit bad writing, but you can't edit a blank page. So schedule time and start writing.

RUTH E. GRIFFIN

Remember always
that to get
through you have
to go through!
And when you get
through, remember
to reach back and
help somebody else.

VICTORIA E. HENDERSON

Life has a way
of allowing us to
experience both
pinnacles and
pitfalls. Embrace
them both and
endeavor to
endure.

ANDREA L. HINES

Authors Up

We are a forum for authors by authors.

Hosted by Andrea L. Hines, Victoria E. Henderson, and Ruth E. Griffin, Authors Up is a weekly internet television show that provides a platform for first-time and established writers to share their work.

In addition to interviews, we feature writing and publishing tips, and a myriad of writing challenges, contests, radio productions and much more. Listen to find your new favorite book, to express yourself, or to simply be entertained.

We air weekly on Sunday night at 7pm EST on SIBN and Facebook Live. You can catch a replay on Saturday evenings at 7pm EST. Watch us anytime on YouTube (like and subscribe!) or download our podcast from your favorite platform.

Find us and follow us online:

 AuthorsUp

authorsupshow

 Authors Up

 bit.ly/AuthorsUp

 Anchor.fm/authorsup